Dear God,
Do Something!

Have you ever known a bully? A bully is someone who picks on you, teases you, or calls you names. Most bullies are just plain mean! But being unkind to a bully doesn't help. If you really want to teach a bully a lesson, you should be NICE! God says that showing kindness and love to your enemy will discourage a mean person's ways. God wants us to love everybody, even bullies.

If your enemy is hungry give him bread to eat; And if he is thirsty, give him water to drink. For doing so you will heap coals of fire on his head. And the Lord will reward you.

Proverbs 25:21-22

Dear God,
It's good to have
team spirit!

But I am bummed out
about losing the big game.
If you give your best
effort and please God with
your actions, it's more
important than winning or
losing. Both teams want
to win. But it is important
to keep a good attitude,
whether you win or lose.
If you win, don't be proud.
If you lose, be sure to
congratulate the other
team, and recognize
their victory. Whether
you win or lose, God wants
you to keep working hard,
to give your all, and to
remain joyful.

The Lord gave and the Lord has taken away;
may the name of the Lord be praised.

Job 1:21

Dear God,

This is sounding better all the time.

God has given you the talent to do a few special things very well. Maybe it's making music on your keyboard, or thinking up clever stories, or kicking a ball over everybody's head. None of those things make you better than anybody else because other people have their own list of abilities. But your talents are a gift from God and using them well is your gift to Him.

Whatever your hand finds to do,
do it with all your might.
Ecclesiastes 9:10

Dear God,
I'm tired of sitting on the side.

You're going to feel left out sometimes. Everyone does. You'll get mad when something doesn't go your way. You'll feel like quitting when something gets too tough. The job of being you can be hard when you're all alone. But you're not really ever alone, because God is always with you. And the times you feel the worst are the times you can know God the best.

The Lord himself ... will never leave you.
Deuteronomy 31:8

Dear God,
A real friend is someone who takes time to listen to you.

It's a whole lot easier to talk than to listen. It's a whole lot more fun to tell what you got for Christmas than to hear what they got. It's a whole lot harder to care what somebody else thinks when you think you haven't been treated fairly. But how great it is to have a friend who'll listen when you feel like talking or to be a friend who listens to what others need to say.

Rejoice with those who rejoice; mourn with those who mourn.

Romans 12:15

Dear God,
I think I'll dress up today ... just in case you've got something special in mind.

Every morning when you push the covers back, you're ripping the wrapper off a shiny, new present, a day not quite like any other you've ever lived before or like any you'll live again. Somehow, God never gets tired of watching the sun come up, seeing the flowers drip with dew, or giving you a day like today full of new things for you to do, to learn, and to enjoy.

Rejoice in the Lord always: and again I say, Rejoice.

Philippians 4:4

Dear God,
Am I listening?

Can you hear God's voice? Sometimes it seems mighty quiet when we need Him the most. But God talks to us in many different ways. He speaks through His written Word, but also in the wonders of our amazing planet and the sound of a baby's laugh. God is always speaking to us. We only have to be still and listen, not only with our ears, but with our hearts, too!

Let the one who is wise heed these things and ponder the loving deeds of the Lord.

Psalm 107:43

Dear God,
Words are wonderful ...
you can even send them
to those you love.

Between that little pink
tongue of yours and
those shiny white teeth,
you can say any word
you want. Your tongue
and your teeth don't
really care what it is.
But your friends do. And
God does. Because when
you say kind and helpful
words, you give your
friends something to talk
about—a friend like you
who really loves them.

For out of the abundance of the
heart the mouth speaketh.

Matthew 12:34

Dear God,

Have you noticed I could do with a little help around here?

Everybody needs help. You can count on God to help you with anything. He will help you because He loves you. Sometimes, He sends friends or family to give you the help you need. Other times, He will help you Himself in the way you need most. Ask for help and God will be happy to be there for you.

Behold! God is my helper! The Lord is with those who uphold my life!

Psalm 54:4

Dear God,
Are You Telling
Me Something?

Dear God,
Are you telling
me something?

Maybe you're walking along
a beach, riding your bike,
or waiting to fall asleep in
your cozy bed, when, all
of a sudden, you feel that
God is trying to tell you
something. Be still and pay
close attention, and you'll
know what the message is!
For example, the constant
whoosh of the waves on
the shore just might be
God's way of whispering,
"I'm always, always here
with you, and that will
never change."

Hear what the LORD says to you…
Jeremiah 10:1

Dear God,

Give me a hint.
Where are you?

I cannot see you. I cannot hear your voice. I am having a rough time following ... please help me find you! When I have difficulty hearing God's voice, I ask God to open my ears. I learn to stay silent. As I quietly listen, the Lord speaks to my heart. I must obey His instructions. If I have a rough time obeying His instructions, I ask God to help me. The Lord quickly answers my call.

If any of you lack wisdom, let him ask of God, that giveth to all men liberally ... and it shall be given him.

James 1:5

Dear God,
We need to talk!

Oh, no! You just made a big mistake. You broke Mom's favorite vase. What should you do? You could tell a lie, or blame your brother or sister. Maybe you should run for the hills. No, facing Mom and telling her the truth will be much better than trying to run or hide. Wrong choices can make you miserable. But no mistake will ever stop God from loving you. He would much rather you tell the truth.

And you shall know the truth and the truth shall set you free.

John 8:32

Dear God,
What do you think?

God takes one good look at you and remembers the day He made your fingers and toes, chose your height and your hair color, put in your own little personality, and smiled at the you He had created. If you had put that much thought and love into something you had made, wouldn't you think it was extra special? That's how God feels about you.

Keep me as the apple of your eye; hide me under the shadow of your wings.

Psalm 17:8

Dear God,
Another adventure!
Let's go!

Moving from house to house, whether it is across town or across the country, is often a stressful time. Sure, you will miss your old friends, but you can trust that God has a bigger vision for your life. When you get settled in your new home, you will meet new and wonderful friends. Think of that! Then you'll have even more friends than you had before!

Trust in the Lord and do good, and thou shalt dwell in the land, and verily thou shall be fed.

Psalm 37:3

Dear God, Do You Have A Minute?

Dear God,
Do you have a minute?

Questions are good. And questions about God are some of the best questions of all. The reason is that the more you find out about God, the more you'll know how much He loves you. You'll find out how to act in any situation. You'll find out what it means to have God as a friend. Grown-ups may not have all the answers, but ask anyway. They might learn something too.

For the Lord giveth wisdom; out of His mouth cometh knowledge and understanding.

Proverbs 2:6

Dear God,

That's it for tonight! Talk to you tomorrow.

Does God ever sleep? How about on Sunday? Did God really create the world in seven days? What's the answer? True? False? I try my best to study and learn. I need God's wisdom to help me understand things. God gives me a healthy mind. When I need the answer to a tough question, I ask God to help me. God's Word tells me to give Him my concerns, because He cares for me. God promises to give me understanding when I ask. God gives me clear thinking and good judgment, especially after a good night of sleep.

He taught me also, and said unto me, Let thine heart retain my words:
Keep my commandments and live. Get wisdom, get understanding: forget it not ...

Proverbs 4:4-5

Dear God,

Every little bit helps! Why do I have to do what Mom says?

It is not always fun making your bed or cleaning your room. But God wants us to obey our parents. God has put your parents in charge of knowing what's best for you. So, the next time your mom asks you to help in the kitchen, do as she asks with respect. You will make your mom happy. You will be pleasing God, too!

Honor thy father and mother as the Lord thy Father has commanded you.

Deuteronomy 5:16

Dear God,

I'll miss him! Why did my fish have to die?

Death is never easy to understand. It is sad to lose a goldfish friend, or any pet. We should remember that God has a plan and a purpose for everything. He knows just the right time for us to say goodbye. He has everything under control. He knows how it feels to be sad, and He wants to bring you joy. Always remember that God loves you and has great things in store for you.

Blessed are those who mourn, for they will be comforted.

Matthew 5:4

Dear God,
Where are you?

Have you ever felt that sick feeling in your stomach when you knew that you were lost? Maybe it was in the supermarket or in the woods. But what a wonderful feeling it is when you've been found again! Whenever you are lost, turn to God for help. He is an expert in this area. He will comfort you and guide you back to safety. Whatever mess you get in, God will help you find your way through.

That the saying might be fullfilled which He spoke, "Of those whom you gave Me, I have lost none."

John 18:9

Dear God,
You know we could do with some ... good news.

Do you ever feel afraid when you think about growing up and getting older? Do you ever get upset when you watch television and see people who have been hurt? Do you ever get nervous when Mom and Dad say a big thunderstorm is coming? Here's some good news—nothing ever catches God by surprise or can keep Him from taking care of you. The reports are in, and being afraid is out.

He shall deliver thee in six troubles.
Yes, in seven there shall no evil touch thee.
Job 5:19

Dear God,
What a day! Thanks!

Each day is a gift from God. I thank God for this gift. I praise God in the morning. I praise God in the afternoon. I praise God in the evening. I praise God for who He is. I thank God for what He does. The Lord is good. The Lord is worthy of my praise. I remember to thank God for at least five things daily: Life, Food, Home, Family, and Friends.

O give thanks unto the Lord; for He is good;
for His mercy endureth for ever.

1 Chronicles 16:34

Dear God,

So I'm having a bad day ... did you ever have one?

Everybody has days that aren't so great, days when things just don't go the best. The real question is: What will you do about your "bad day"? Will you be mad about it? Or will you learn from it? Or will you praise God anyway? Every day is a special gift from Him. He wants you to rejoice and be glad in the day He made for you! Even if it isn't a perfect day, no day will ever really be bad!

This is the day that the Lord has made. Let us rejoice and be glad in it!

Psalm 118:24

Dear God,

He needs help! Help me to help others.

It makes me sad when I see people who do not have a home. What can I do to help them? One of the best ways to help people is to pray for them. God watches out for every person, even if he or she does not have a home. Homeless people are in special need of our prayers. Ask God to help those who are in need. We can show God's love to all people by praying for them and sharing our blessings with them.

He raises the poor from the dust and lifts the needy from the ash heap; He seats them with princes, with the princes of his people.

Psalm 113:7-8

Dear God,
Next to you ... he's my best friend!

Cats and dogs are great friends and companions. They make you laugh and keep you entertained. You take good care of your pets because you love them. Just as you are the master of your pet, God is the master of all of us. Your pet trusts you to feed and shelter it. You can put your trust in God. He will always take care of you!

He shall feed His flock like a shepherd; He shall gather the lambs with His arm, and carry them in His bosom, and shall gently lead those that are with young.

Isaiah 40:11